Apparitionist

Whitenails

Indoor Fighting Press

Front Cover: "Blue Screen" by Andrew Salgado

Beers London

Introduction

The illusionist, claimed Gary Gygax in one of his now dust-shrouded tomes masquerading as even dustier-shrouded tomes, is one of a cohort who "forms a sub-class of magic users, and in most respects they conform to the characteristics of the latter."

The disillusionist, sings poet Steve Kilbey in a song reaching back a quarter of a century, suffers since "the top half of his body is a corpse. His gold won't buy him sleep, his poverty runs so deep. In winter he cracks, in summer he warps."

And what of the apparitionist?

What does the apparition mean to you, it might be asked? Do you will it into existence yourself? Do you hide from it? Do you know it when you see it? Would you know how to react if so?

Whitenails provides to you a perspective that might be the apparition conjured, or described, or sensed. But are you the apparitionist yourself, when you are caught in the tangle, or the warp and woof?

It may be distant, it may sidle up to you even now. Are you entranced? Or do you simply head for an entrance?

Either way, turn the page, and shift from where you are now.

— *Ned Raggett, San Francisco, November 2017*

Shell House, Polperro

Frontispiece for two doors oblique to each other, viewed squarely
Is seamed by the perron that enables, however rarely,
A person to exit and, should they wish, climb and re-enter
The house through a porch on the noble floor, skewing momenta
Of a life in progress and a life's totality reviewed,
So the mind queries among coat hooks, and once more when endued
With a power to separate, why the body diverted;
Viewed from one side is unfolded, and shows me in hair-shirted
Recursion climbing the steps, grey steps not visible square on,
To cover off a possible way to leave that, so far, none
May have taken: I leave through the ground floor door a second time,
And go to the Blue Peter Inn; still I see just one sublime
Passage, despite wavering interpolations, coalesce,
One pass, resolutely reformatory, as I assess
My life. A face, unfamiliar, presents itself to me –
This review of life must be independent of memory –
Face of a girl who is perhaps 11 or 12 years old;
I with true wakefulness, as one who is over the threshold,
See this child, and note that her hair is blonde beneath the sedge hat
She is wearing, but still cannot recognise her or see that
This could pertain to my life even; and her voice as she speaks –
Its quality, its colour and the curious way it peaks –
Is strange to me also: "You abandoned me," says she, softly,
And leaves me brooding over her statement's import whilst I see
Myself continue, an apparitionist, towards the Blue
Peter Inn. This girl and my excursion are contiguous through
One pass, a single conjuncture.

Picnicking in Hook Meadow with a Family from Nice, I Connect

Aorist, I loved—how long for?
Was love fixed, or like the tides
That laved the shore
By quotidian divides?

Pica, I partook of ore
Concealed by esculent airs;
Penugem, saw,
Up close, the raspberries' hairs;

Felt no hunger for those four
Pulps atop my fingers, splayed,
But craved rapport,
And so, merrivore, I played.

Papillon

I step over robin fledglings in the garden, and help the old man pull the
hinge from a rotten door.
Aye Steph, that I once shunned you makes my suffering, as I wait at the
British Embassy's postern, more.
You were right, I struggled when you left for Nice; my impassiveness from
which I presumed to further draw
Became redundant, and I grew ashamed; and now, pray that you are alive,
and not grieving for your children or
Your husband, I hope the consul will not reveal who enquired after you—I
who did not esteem your
Parting admonition. I assent to its sentiments now, remembering how on
the day before
You moved from Crondall, seven years ago, you were perturbed. Age
advanced, my hair is ash of aigremore,
But care for you is vibrant, and yet belied by a consul's triage that factors in
how I forswore
Our kindredship, to recommend my solicitude be allocated a non-priority
score.

Nurmalso

Who is that man with greying hair, who enters alone, appendix to the flock
finds a pew unoccupied in the South Aisle, restricted of view, does not
kneel or seem to know the patterns of worship, says "no" to collection by
simpering and showing an empty hand, appears baffled when the faithful
are invited to extend peace, and then keeps staring throughout the final
hymn, surprised, pensive, at the back of the head of the woman who turned
around to shake his hand?

I am that man.

Yearly, the squire calls at my house, exhorts continued fealty
By renewing my subscription to the parish magazine.
Dearly dunned, and by no compulsion other than my frailty,
I have come to this service at midnight, grateful for the screen
Of ramified arches. I nearly stayed at home.

The Intercessor

Visiting my mum today, I quietly opened the front door and snuck up on her like I used to do. In those moments, as I waited in the kitchen for her to turn around so I could make her jump, I realised she is 73, and I very quietly snuck all the way back out and rang the doorbell.

My dog, Larkin, is staring at the wall behind my shoulder. I say the command, "basket", and she leaves the room. It is something to do with his unawareness that makes the back of my little boy's head so dear, the hairline ending in three soft triangles, and there my love is allowed to pool undetected in the undulations of his nape, as he plays with his paper people on the windowsill; and I am thinking about how it would be to appear spontaneously to someone who is alone, a stranger who is feeling despondent, and as their counterfeit angel, confer genuine succour, and be convincing enough to inform a lasting faith. Perhaps, in order to mitigate the shock of seeing me in a vision, I should pre-empt my arrival by voicing something in the stillness? I would say it lovingly. I practice saying things lovingly across my own ears and conclude that the utterance I find most consoling is my name, evocative of mornings in my childhood when a parent or one of my sisters woke me up with hushed mien. Surely, a power enabling me thus to visit someone would not leave me at a disadvantage, but would also allow me to intuit the stranger's name moments before I manifest myself?

I had three dreams in which I interviewed contrasting intercessors. In the first dream, the Unknown Soldier told me of a district he had been detailed to control.
"I met a starving boy in Yarmouk who forsook
His future existentially:
'Make chemical weapons smell of bread,
Or can you stop the cavalry?' –
I could not."
The next was an angel of grief. I asked her where she had roved afore. She replied,
"This evening with a woman as she walked through Hook
Meadow, to the graveyard where she
Placed a lantern, glowing faintly red,
In a section especially
For children.
I heard her whisper 'My baby, who sleeps in the February cold,
Here is your night light,' and I prayed for her, was all I could do."
Eftsoons, having gone to my bed one night tearful with anger, I dreamt of

the final presence. Whilst I was calmed by the equanimity of his bearing, with his hands in his pockets he explained to me that he lives, is still living, but that he is often called on to give reassurance to those who have passed over, which alarmed me. "And by your showing up now, am I to infer that I am dead?" I asked. "No," he said, "I only thought you might be interested to hear about my role." "OK, so tell me, do *you* feel you are able to help people?" "I do. I tell them that they need not fear God." Although "not fear God" was what I understood, the sound I heard was "Hoxmarch ipamis".

Following that third dream, I spent all the next day feeling nauseous yet still hungry. Each time I ate I did so knowing that there was a possibility it wouldn't stay down, and so deliberately sought out food I have never really liked, sacrificing it to the inevitable future association with the pain of being sick. I had butternut squash for lunch and cheese crackers for tea, doing what was necessary to insure against a loss of my predilection for viands, quinoa and porridge.

O the ordeal of existence!, joy's refrain thwarted each time in its nascence by tremendous retches, and if there is consciousness after it, the tragedy is that we will associate our loved ones with that ordeal and they will be marred by this association, and we will have an aversion to them and to e'er going back into the horror of life. But maybe we do come back with alacrity, un-protesting and without fear, because, after the final intercessor has hinted that Love is eternal, all its adjuncts – the name of a person, along with all queasy memories of husbands, wives, children and friends – are taken away.

Brother-in-law, there is already someone looking tenderly at the back of your head, but I want to be there after your death, to remind you of Love and to take away your memories. First, I would remove your most cynical one.

Your memory of me, age eleven doing an impression of Rik Mayall,
Is reductive propaganda, and is not nursed fondly.
You make yourself appear magnanimous, whilst manufacturing the portrayal
Of me as a stolid adult, through your account of me
Telling Doctor Doctor jokes, Christmas 1982. Only I, a wary
Pragmatics-ferret and precariat on the cosine of the line of loyal
Sisterly affection, 31 years after those skits,
Only I see how details of a child's exuberance are used as a foil
To your characterisation of me, now, as a schiz

oid malingerer, showing flat affect, caught obsequiously in the orbits
Of profitless "poetic" tangents.

Your life has ended. You are alone in a quiet waiting room. You can hear
some background sounds, children playing and someone shaking a drawer
loose from a desk in another room. And then you hear a voice, my voice,
saying your name. You cannot see me.

And your name is the nature of my intercession,
That name you responded to to the end;
I am melancholy enough to say it so that you comprehend,
So that you are not startled.
I am loving enough and migrainous enough,
And whilst I have always been somewhere on the spectrum –
Too mad to hold down a job, too serious, bovine, almost sinister –
I am well suited to say your name now,
And you understand that it is the last time you will hear it;
And no one applauds after the first act of Parsifal,
And they re-recorded Gram Parsons's vocals;
And Love is the hapax here, Love is the palimpsest
For your name. Hoxmarch ipamis.

Prepared Eulogy

"If you start counting now," my mother would say, as we waited in the car park, "he's sure to be with us before you reach one hundred." We would start, each number intoned teasingly so as to tempt my father to turn up. It seemed to us, as children, that we could verifiably influence the duration of our wait: before my sisters and I got to one hundred, usually towards the higher nineties, my father, commuting back from work, would emerge from the train station.

Once, in life, my father failed to come back,
Delaying with demurrage in death.
Homing, had we counted hundreds more,
As inveiglers of schedulers, of rail track
And of fate, and appealed under breath
In thousands, then, to a causal law,
We could not have delivered him to emerge.
He left work when it was dark, timely
For his tube, were he only to carve
A thoroughfare over the verge – small verge,
Might as well have been a steppe, that he
Expected would trim or even halve
His journey, but he strode into a crossbar,
Horizontal, hidden and head high,
Which split his spectacles at the ridge.
While he journeyed across that verge, veering far
As the hospital, for stitches, I
Was counting fruitlessly to abridge
His journey home.

Conjuncture

The headmistress of my infants school in Wickford wore her hair erect in buns, bun upon bun and depending from a scaffold of outrage commensurate to Victorian vestiges. In my mind, they seemed to build whenever she was made angry, and I would make my family laugh with my impersonation of her, saying "bundle, bundle, bundle" whilst putting one fist atop another over my head. Each "b" would be pronounced more explosively as I planted my fists higher and higher in an act that resembled some kind of drawing straws sortition.

As a five-year-old in the year of the Queen's silver jubilee, I made Mrs Goodman angry a lot. I was sent to her office frequently, once for strangling myself during playtime until I went crimson. She had been given an account of the incident by a playground monitor, but Mrs Goodman told me that I must demonstrate to her exactly what happened, and without hesitation I put my hands either side of my neck, so that my elbows pointed at her as she sat at her desk, a picture of the Queen behind her head, and I held my breath. After watching me for several seconds, my elbows wavering with accusing zeal in the vicinity of the monarch, that dutiful subject, Mrs Goodman, cried out a shrill "Stop". Top knot atop top knot, she wrested my shoes from my feet and made me stand in just my socks on a copy of the Daily Mail outside her office, a bizarre punishment, which she often used, presumably designed to humiliate and degrade.

Starting from the age of 14 years, in an effort to iron out my curls, I would spit into my hand and wet the back of my hair, before sitting upright for a timed-hour in an armchair, my head pressed continuously against the headrest. As family members moved around the living room, I sat still, pressing my head and neck back fixedly, double-chinned and with strangulated voice, looking ahead even when I was speaking with someone standing behind me.

Over a period of months, compressed by the occipital region of my skull the grey velveteen upholstery of the headrest became matted in the centre, turned slightly purple, like clouds at dusk over marshland; and it was all in vain, all in vain and for nothing that I sat fixated in my shorts, perspiring, like some ruddy-thighed Abraham Lincoln, trying to straighten, while others moved easily around me.

The Bribe

By collocation-contingent slang,
My barnet's fringe contrary to bang
Is puffy; is now, was ever thus,
When, never more conscious that a bus
Was travelling down hill, I watched my
Vomit tidal-meander, whence I
Was sitting at the back, down between
Rows of seats, heard a voice intervene:
"Oh my God, he's pissed himself!" The girl,
Mistaking my spirit level hurl
For urine in alerting her friend,
Was not much older than me. A bend
Coarsened my sense of the sloping road
And grey deck of a bus to forebode
The years that would pursue my 12th year.
Bruce's dad had bought me 12 pints of beer
The night before. My last memory
Prior to passing out finally
On the carpet was of his warm breath
Pronouncing a stifling shibboleth,
Blowing into my mouth, blowback dope;
And as the road continued to slope,
And I vomited more of that clear
Beer, I could recall stumbling in fear
Up the stairs, having once awoken,
To find, in malign dark, the token
Of a bed. Two weeks hence, because Bruce
And I were wilfully too obtuse
Within our friendship to acknowledge,
As we played near the Old Vicarage
In Grantchester, that we were not fond
Of each other, we laboured this bond,
Set afloat on the pond the canoe
That his dad had given me, when two
Boys came up to us. "You can't do that,"
Said one. "Fuck off," I said. Bruce sat
In the boat, amused by the fervid
Objection. "You're Jeffrey Archer's kid,"
He proffered to the one who had piped,
Who pulled at the mooring, and I swiped
It back, and Bruce fell in.

The Manual for the ZX81

GOTO non-recent abuse, and 35 years on
It seems that instead of typing 'PRINT "Play Player 1"'
In the BASIC program for that space invaders game
(Why should disclosing this make me, the abused, feel shame?),
He evidently typed in 'PRINT "Prepare to be bummed!!!"'

If by reading, in retrospect, the manual for
The ZX81, tracing what he did before
My visit to his house, commands he must have typed in,
I have fought him off once more, what of children akin,
But children I fear, subsequent I fear, who succumbed?

I write to the NSPCC: He was 16,
I was 10. He had set that message to flash on screen
Each time I lost a life; I repeat it verbatim,
Testifying to what is puerile and makes me squirm,
Sinister when his scheming and aggression are summed.

The Irresponsible Revolutionist

How will I, as irresponsible revolutionist, militate against the rolling back of
historical progress?
I cannot assume in advance that anything will change, nor do I anticipate
acceptance – there is no prolepsis –
Am alive to rain of the thaw, chugging dragsaw, far as Bransgore, and pass
over what I shall do, no burden to confess.
I read books by glimpsing. All my adult life, I have done so. I shall live thus.
Raindrops fall from the leaves only, and yet this
Approximate rain, in its velocity and distribution, convinces me, even as I
walk in the dry spaces
In between each tree, that it is raining, raining out of sky. Disclaiming, I
hear the chugging dragsaw, and do not admit
Even to myself what I will do.

Old Edinburgh, New Sheffield

Burke and Hare's defence was Jekyll and Hyde,
That drink had made their good characters base,
Was palliative just as Hare had tried
To smooth horror from the dead mute boy's face
After breaking his back over Burke's knee.

Northern Powerhouse, by misgovernment,
Apostates are drinking in Wetherspoon's;
A girl with a sign, "Free Encouragement
Or Free Disabusals"; and I hear noon's
Bells in Fargate and throughout Black Swan Walk.

Fountains add to this feeling of leisure,
So too the currentous orbs and the trees
From Tasmania, but by myth, measure
Or murder, the people who no one sees
Are those who can afford to lose their faith.

And this empty glass that has amplified
My iPod's songs, now amplifies the boy's
Gasps; and I hear his voice ring from inside
Fox Hole Cave; odd virgin voice that alloys
Arthur's Seat, Park Hill and here, High Wheeldon;

Shashing noise of sobs with curtailed egress,
Calling. A life mute in mute poverty,
His gasps are residual, to address
Me by name the boy must have finally
Found a voice; and I am presumptuous:

When friendly instructional couplets
On disposing of sanitary things,
Displayed above the cisterns in toilets,
Have readership greater than mine, why rings
His voice in this chamber for me? He speaks,

And instead tenders a criticism:
"Why do you lament in such ambience
Of love, sing of Apparitionism
When so learned and without encumbrance?"

The Road to Damascus, via Miami

False-casting inclined imitative of the midge snuffles the sconce;
My circumventive theory of mind provokes a frigid response
In those for whom lies are valueless catacombs, catacombs, sealed,
And who do not note fundamental wordings in Hayden, Masefield,
Keats and Cummings as properties of truth. I felt this jarring
Rigor by false-cast in its other meaning, when someone, barring
The sheath I was wearing, lay there suddenly tense. The sheath repulsed
Just as my making things up would do; and the artist sprawls convulsed
Upon the sand dunes, hugging himself so that the lower left flap
Of the tweed jacket bequeathed by his father makes elegant gap
Of grief, riding over towards his right shoulder.

Godshill

The wind was cold, but elicited fascinating canopy mechanics, starting in the morning with a stray open umbrella, inscriber of arcs with a fledgling's instincts, moving by its leaning in the courtyard.

The Gong

Had I been told at two years old that I alone made ordure,
So that for solace summoned I the tiller of soil, Georgia,
Whose sanitary raking rid me not of shame in going,
In credence, when I shared this urge with others before knowing,
Then I would have reason, something that accounts for empathy,
Tenderness at the notion of inevitability.

Experiment with a Sunbeam

There is a sun spot on the floor in the doorway, farthest facet of a sunbeam that penetrates through the window of an adjacent room. Slowly closing the door to my bedroom, I watch to see what will happen when it reaches the spot. I expect the beam will be blocked, but instead it bounces off the back of the door and remains on the floor as a reflected beam. The glint then moves ahead of the closing door, which cannot gain on it.

Like the sunbeam constant on the closing door,
Glimpsing its reflection moving on the floor
With an independent will,
Enticingly towards the threshold sill,
I am thus barred, divided by rejection,
A constant desiring its reflection,
Clothed by the self's conspiracy,
In so nude a bum in the mirror see
The object of desire.

The Marbling Tree

Winds erode soils to move augers to make square guitars,
Discovered beneath the tree that marbles skies of March;
Mortice chisels brought here by susurrant leverage.
An obscure figure of speech, lacuna privilege,
Allows me to think, and you to speculate, in free
Parenthesis.   That is left me,
Winds erode soils to move.
I exist, ellipsis, before the marbling tree,
Part ghost, with my jogging pants billowing risibly,
Your construct in the absence of my thoughts' furnishing.
Lacuna privilege solicits speculating,
That in this gusty groove
Where the augers gather, beneath the marbling tree,
I might exist, jogging pants ballooning about me.

The Suggestion of a Standing Being

Upon which inferences seesaw from spectre to score,
Some shade, inert, extending recumbently from the fore
On the track ahead of me, rises, stands as revenant,
Lies as gouge made by a tractor's wheel in the sediment,
Again seems upright, then once more flat on the plane, to roil—
Hard to tell, till this hatch false-flipping on perception's coil
Moves off! It steals, as I run towards it, into the wood's
Yardley clearing, where lurk more anamorphic shapes in hoods
Of iridescent, black oil. A trumpet sound fills the sky,
Leaves fall at once. They call to me, "What is it you want?" "I
Am just looking around," I dissemble. Once more, they call,
And I cower down low, for a hatch's stature is tall,
Is tall, or flat and angled away—it is hard to tell.
You will reassure yourself, but it is hard to dispel
The suggestion of a standing being, who holds, ahead
On the track, in between the lobes of its morbid wall bed,
Those who give chase.

Retroreflection

Saying "Hello there?" out loud to myself, stentorian, conditions me into thinking someone is calling through the letterbox. They have found me. Disturbing my own quiet, with my voice they have found me; retroreflector, catalingual eidolon, calling extempore.

Old Woking

Our house in Old Woking was a non-house among the shambles,
Opposite the church where campanologists pulled random ropes.

My wife was in Germany, and I was looking after my parents' dog. On the morning of New Year's Day, walking past the rehab clinic at the end of the road, I heard loud sobbing. A man was standing alone, facing the high brambles at the entrance to the footpath. I could see his shoulders rising and falling with each sob. As I got nearer, the dog began to bark, and I remember saying something like "Are you OK, mate? Mate?" It was an odd expression for me to use, mate, and a silly question. He didn't turn around. He didn't answer. He just kept sobbing.

These Non-coronate Rhymes

Whence came the novelist
When the sun was eclipsed?
And Old Dutch ketchup chips?

Sometimes it gets so eclipsey we are sent home,
To families unfamiliar in the gloom,
Where cookie jars' press-to-seal lids k'hubbalhum,
Like that sound one makes between fluffing a sentence
And retrying it, because nothing in tristesse
And loon of migraine is slick; and those pedants
By stinted dares on a miniature ingres sheet
Cannot see how I paint thus for the synesthete,
Using catachresis and transferred epithet,
But they distinguish between Sitter and Subject
When memory is the primary referent.
Rejecting the confined cosmos of these pendants
Of chrome, I will paint a memory: M. Imrie.

He had a holy look.

On Discovering the Poetry of Ebenezer Elliott

The river shares its course incontinently, for fate,
And as the softest rock erodes at its eager rate,
I was first taught Hardy, then Wordsworth and muse, his kin.
Not being taught yet learning of Celia Dropkin
Erodes a harder rock anterior to schooling,
Whence then a waterfall descends, which never pooling
In prejudice is callow in liberation's lock.

My didactic Hippocrene assayed to erode rock
In an artist whose work I had previously bought,
And I made my investment unsafe, because I taught
By wheedling. Had that artist investigated my
Poems cheerfully, without my testament that I
Exist, he might not have given Bowie a hooked nose
In his new gestural portrait that otherwise owes
Little to his flight to evade my political
Freight.

Lines written at the base of High Wheeldon

This evening, my fate became entangled with Samantha Morton's and thereof I was granted free admittance to a John Cooper Clarke gig in Bakewell, thanks to his manager, Phil Jones.
Two days before, I had visited the churchyard of St. Mary Magdalene in Tanworth-in-Arden, contemplated, by the oak tree, mortality in being so close to Nick Drake's bones;
The trudge of blood, hlud, in my throat, my dog's coat, soft as days-old grate-ash, tangible only when my knuckles were pitched and then glancing-kissed by fingertips and wrist sensitive to pulver.
No one knows how I take up space, how my fate precludes their own.

Below Solomon's Temple

"I find, if I shake my balls," grabs my attention as the opening to a statement, spoken as if into my ear. It makes me glance up.

The voice that sounded so close belongs to a man who is actually some way off, apparently illustrating his words with an unfortunate mime. He and a woman are approaching from above, descending along one of the permutations of pathway. Although I can see them, it seems that they can't yet see me sat here in the valley, veiled as I am by mist. It must also be that the mist is increasing the amplitude of his interjection, his ejaculation so to speak, which continues, "it makes me go stiffer."

His display of ingenuity in overcoming impotence is suspended when he notices me sat on this bench, suddenly distinct among buttercups, their yellow at once accenting the white mist. I hear him say to the woman, quieter but still surprisingly discernible at this distance: "Do you think he heard me?"

Tan Hill

When darkness shrouds the summit peace like pollen spreads.
Cows that glow like dying bonfires rest on briary beds.
Lost lovers with laryngitis pitch their songs of woe
Over Arkengarthdale peaks and into Keld below.
The inn is out and out the highest in the land,
A pole-vault from the sun, a haven for the tanned.
Walkers swap their scary tales
Of ghouls and farmers on the dales,
But if a corpse in old West Burton
Really curtsied seems uncertain.
And does a man from Reeth keep demons in his barn?
No one yet has ever dared to verify that yarn.

Conjuncture

Sitting on some steps waiting to go on a tour of NBC studios in Rockefeller
Center
(It is not what I bore);
Six thousand miles from home, a fan of The Fall; anorexia and migraine
were my new impedimenta
(but how much I bore, stoically);
I was 18 in New York, and Frank O'Hara meant nothing to me
(assimilating pain as if it were an extension of childhood).
I was the first of my generation to go
To New York.

I seldom washed. I did not change. I slept in my bomber jacket.
A blue culture formed on my scrotum. I now realise that it
Was fabric, in fact, shed by my underwear. I ate just one jam
Sandwich each day. At 18, I would walk along the River Cam
Remembering how I used to deliberately fall in when my
Parents took us punting as kids.

Tinea Capitis and a Recollection of Three Letters

When I was looking for work after graduating, NatWest closed my account suddenly. That week I received three letters. The first was a letter from the local surgery informing me that I had been struck off my doctor's practice list. Next came the letter from the bank, explaining that it was costing more money than was in the account to keep it open. As it turned out, a member of the surgery's administration staff had made an error, easily resolved with a single phone call, but the incontrovertible letter from the bank affected me deeply.

In my mind the bank's decision betrayed a broader appraisal of my prospects. I was only 21. It was damning, and dejection, despite a switch to Lloyds that same afternoon, despite all the subsequent years, lingers, lingers long after that week in 1993, a week when it felt like my health and finances were being dismantled following certification of my death, a week when a third letter informed me that my application to be a marketing assistant for a firm selling fire-protection paint had been unsuccessful.

Alas, there is no money in poetry and so the bank's expediency, but for its lack of kindliness, appears to be vindicated; and I am here, at a place where morbidity and mortality meet, 1.46 am, taking photos of my feet. My scalp half beset with ringworm, as I am half jaundiced by the physic, with yellowing eyes and clay stools, I make a study of feet (the redeemer's feet?). For a malady so trivial I take overmuch, overmuch.

The Stairwell

The rota, which required junior library personnel
To alternate duties, assigned me to that dreary stairwell
Once a month; and there I would sit, arschhungrig, barring the way,
While going through readers' handbags on the green leather inlay
Of my desk, looking, supposedly, for a countdown timer
And wires, before gazing at the rear of each female climber
Of those stone steps. For one morning of one day, one week in four,
I would sit alone in the stairwell below the corridor
That led to the Reading Room; from below saw contours imply
How soft is the flesh beneath the eaves, the soffit of a thigh.

Cogito-glot

In my career as a sound engineer, such as it was, I worked on two episodes of a TV show with a person who habitually and pompously steered every conversation round to his preferred discipline, in this case oenology. I once mentioned to him that I grew up in Cambridge, and he reacted to my words like they were chewy tannin. Swilling my folly, splurging it didactically back into a spittoon, he briskly got me thinking that perhaps I didn't grow up there after all; and I learned that the Anchor pub is not in fact on Silver Street, and that red wine is kept in obfusc bottles.

Inner speech is accompanied by muscular movements in the larynx; cogito-glot.
I suffer in-ear, each morning, each morning, translating myself, and when sleep's gussets blot
Haematuria.

Creepy-crawly Decal

I discover blood in my underwear between voidings. I make an
appointment to see my doctor. He gives me a sample bottle to fill.
Furtively, I slip it, unlabelled, into the pocket of someone on the school
run.

The Scapegoat

At ten past eight,
And for two undifferentiated whiles,
I vacillate,
Migraine beneath my occipital condyles,
In this passageway,
Uncertain of where I am in the sequence
Of my day.
AM or PM? I, whom, in their frequence,
Phantoms affirm,
First stamp one foot squarely off-gait on the floor,
Pivot, infirm,
And then stride as purposefully as before,
But the other way.

Narrowband

Years 1 to 17: all een
Years 18 to 34: all null
Years 35 to 45: all een

A pie, Low Saxon, up high on my skull,
Through a lifetime's noise, either "een" or "null"
Notch each year – remnants of a lifetime's noise.

"Een" is happy and "null" is not, up high,
At the apex of the sutures, then I
Felt for one weary width no worthy joys.

And how long and wide, all null, this next block?
Foregone, does my outré confession shock
Those who loved me in years after the boy's

Notches were made? I was not happy, friend,
In our time. These blocks of een and null bend
Like a triskelion's legs, when, in poise,

This next block is coming.

The Cantabrigian

Off-centre, I am moved like a string-climbing toy weevil though she displaces
Me laterally onto one thigh, so that by tugging one string
Of my lust while letting the other rise, she ratchets the part that debases
My image of her to the wing;

That part of me which daydreams to appraise almost anybody I might know,
Ascribing one of three sexual acts to perform in cases
Of far-fetched strandedness, only one, leant a frisson by the two I forgo,
By their stricture leaving traces.

Such reveries of being marooned, and introversion when it replaces
Globalisation, of being reconciled to consensual
Acts desirous of incidental milieu, when democracy outpaces
Our options, of eventual

Mutual impulses in associates to soothe in their isolation,
Such reveries impair connectedness.

I Do Not Write Of Love For You

I rinse my hand briefly under the tap – lifting the toilet lid gave me a slight sense of having condensation on my fingertips – and the water is kept running to mask the sounds of my bowel movement. After using the rinsed hand to wipe myself, the tissue paper adheres to my damp fingers, preventing me from disposing of it; shaking it makes it hang down momentarily, like a tired festoon, which then falls onto the floor beside the toilet bowl.

Gloating at stale readdressers
Of love, I lengthen, in lieu
Of hypothetic successors
Hazarding poems for you,
Shadows beneath my beetling verse.
Groat, with likeness of the swain –
Let it be muled with the obverse
Die of a coin from my reign.

Lines on Ettington Park

When I was drunk and fingery in a clinch,
Athwart my wife's flesh with the same reverse-pinch
I use to enlarge things on my iPhone's screen –
Dissolute, nails untrimmed – my eyes were not keen,
Wont to hide as one who feels undeserving;
But now I sit with her in the Great Drawing
Room of the Ettington Park Hotel, where in
Celadon surrounds a strategy to win
Salgado's painting at auction emerges,
And something inside me reaches out, surges
Out from my temple and into the sour
Air: a child's pronated hand, or art's power
To reconcile, disincarnate before me,
Limpid, in phase with my own precarity.
Disincarnate art's power to reconcile,
Is my soul, divested of body, tactile
To your touch? Outside of life and odious
Culture, out of phase with death and Proteus,
You remain a child in perpetuity:
Is your hand an aura, tantalisingly,
Of my own hand, or if lowered, might it feel?
For so long, for so long, I have felt less real,
And now, by your presence, this sense is affirmed:
Have I cheated constant changing patterns termed
Of Proteus forever, or will I go
Back? The intermediary, Salgado,
Shall not suppress what is colourful, nor I
Suppress those sparks in shade cast memetic by
Ong's arboreal hat that moves bough to bough,
Bowlering. Milestones, attained, are worthless now,
As you glide, wizened, not stepping, nor speaking.

Bulletin's Clock

When the fool made a joke at midnight, dialled a humour field leaden,
Lessors of bunkers and leaders amenable to Armageddon
Were ensconced among the paintings of angels on pendentives and domes.
Lower-income families unable to afford the rent on their homes
Were the butt of the joke; its teller, a wag, made capital of art,
Invested, irradiated, and soon the artists would perforce part
From the districts they had made vibrant, Bed-Stuy and Mitte and Hackney.

Felt beneath the bedstead protects a walnut floor; and by irony
And ionising design, a painting, created here when this space
Was still a studio, since bought by a bourgeois who would replace
The painter as tenant, is now mounted above the bed with its frame
Oriented to accentuate the floorboards' grain, not to declaim
Against the joke at midnight, but with neat, anodyne irony
To post-exist. The lacing-stain of paint that seeded itself wildly
On the old chipboard floor is gone, but a presence loath to disconnect
Will stay, the artist's impulse, a domovoi, taking on the aspect
Of the tenant-dilettante, greis, greis, yet keening an imperative
Dissonant from its alike: "When the fool makes a joke at midnight, live,
Do not forbear to live."

Other at the Vernissage

Venoms, emblems, figures fragment,
With Balkanised encadrement;
A white admiral's wings pulsate
Faintly on my back –
A barricade to isolate,
For who would trespass on the weight
Of wings, in onerous catchment
Of a maniac?

Other, here at the vernissage,
Where smaller frames through static charge
Affix to a primary work,
Titled Lazarus,
My soul is alate, a bulwark,
While my physical self is murk,
The bulk of my shoulders is large
Yet a nothingness.

Epanorthosis, pulse, nay, force,
Holding an irresistible course
At death, was countered, as forthtold
When Lazarus rose.
I leave and head over to Old
Street. The autumnal air is cold,
And within the station's concourse,
Leaving its repose,

The butterfly finds my shoulder
And notice, then, of its holder;
Whereupon, smoothing epaulette
To mind it clearer,
Careful not to unseat it yet
Expeditious, I weave to get
Back to the gallery; colder
And nearer, nearer.

The Quiet Man

Jaundiced in the jason'd months, adjuncts anent my purpose by a stillness venting,
I am the quiet man, unanent, whom adjacent maths of a me is dementing.
A quantum bomb in a different universe enacts all the options at once,
So that I lift keys from the hook in the hall at the moment that I ensconce
The keys, at the moment I tickle them whilst they are hanging; or rather, not I,
But that me who siphons the aboutness from me and every other me by
Being zero and one as well as all other numbers simultaneously.
Yet these ciphers in my adjuncts, like the al-iajaaz of Nizar Qabbani
Writing of his homeland, hint at a grief made ineffable by options vacuum.
Jaundiced by course of oral Nizoral, I am the quiet man, unanent, whom
Adjacent maths of a me is dementing.

Blue Screen
(On twice reading that Brian Matthew had just died, on the 5th and the 8th of April)

When did he die? Somewhere, in some place, the family shared three fewer days with Brian Matthew;
It separates from this place, where the family stole
Three further days; but I feel that I too was there, am suddenly here, now, rogue to the curfew,
While outside my window, at a passing place, the whole
Side of a waiting van is blue, reflects into my room, and all furnishings take on its hue,
But not my green greatcoat, nor the grey fibres that roll
From its revers into the ends of my grown hair.

I write for the desk, till Amhai's largesse pays the toll;
You discriminate not arbitrarily, nor out of hate, but to fit the hat of virtue –
Conformiter for a disposable pulp sick bowl.

Apparitionism's Progenitor

My hip shunts into the waist-high garden gate, but my hand reaching over fails to release
The bar from the outswinging latch, and so my body swivels unbuckled, bringing surcease
To my introspection, over the top. I am upside down, doing a headstand, gazing
At the strip of wood that prevents leaves from entering beneath the gate. Autumn is coming.
I shall continue to meet secretly with that muse, simile, with whom I apprenticed,
Talk trustingly to the taproot, pity, make quiet but unconstrained studies of my fist.

Study of Fists

A dog being walked vaults over the bridge wall. Hauling hands wrung pale by the vertical lead dehisce, dehisce — Study of fists, little hairs on a finger, singed by a flame that licked up the side of a saucepan, are curled like copper shavings, as the dog revolves above the purple hues of the rapids.

Atlas

I can only settle in a position that injures me. Lying prone, each voiced exhalation a soothing groan, I bring my hand underneath my body, bend it forwards and use my outer wrist to apply pressure to my tummy. I have fallen asleep this way only to be roused by an ache in my hand, and have not been able to pluck my guitar strings properly for three months until the tendons have healed. Despite this, I still do it; my fingers generally tremble, dexterity is never quite recovered, and it sometimes feels like I am re-learning to hold a pencil.

As a boy, I would fall asleep with my neck flat against the headboard. The rim of the headboard would be wedged between the topmost vertebrae, so that the globe of my head tilted back onto the wall. I think that some gradual realignment may have occurred over the years, where there are nerves and arteries, because I now walk with such imbalance.

The human flesh miasma encumbers
A pledge to increase policing numbers.
I cannot, cannot as one who lumbers
Abroad,
Aggregate avoirdupois of slumber's
Headboard
Bear; the sky and the oceans it umbers
Bear.

Conjuncture

Deprived of Perridge Pale for nearly two years following a regrettable exchange with the landlady of The Flowerpots Inn (she accused me of drinking takeout pints on the premises), I think my not inconsiderable loquaciousness on Friday afternoon had as much to do with the excitement of being reacquainted with this superior sup's apricot-like aroma as with its alcohol content.

As we sat in the garden together, I told my wife about a man I had worked with at Soho Studios, how he would slide his hand subconsciously down the back of his jeans when asked by a runner what he wanted for lunch, and then palpate in between his buttocks, presumably to examine the state of his anus before committing himself to spicy cuisine.

Perridge Pale ale, sole cultural experience left me,
By which, I concede it was impetuous to cry "calumny!"
When the landlady was simply concerned that I stay in the fold.

They spring interventions, united in their design to stymie
The eloquence of my memoir – someone claims without irony,
"My husband is in the public eye." My intercessor forth told
Of this desolateness when she spoke supplications and when she
Sang me songs as a boy: "Be kind, be bold, let your candour be
Like a trier drawn unflinchingly from a squat pillar of cheese.
The resulting cylinder's structure and veined pattern will not please
Everyone, and they would have you stick your trier into coy curds,
But then you should make no attempt to ingratiate through your words,
As you will, as you must, with the landlady of The Flowerpots."

Please understand what is left me – ale that smells of apricots,
When my latitude to write is removed, when my rhymes are all gone.

With Differs Confined

When out walking along the footpaths with my dog, it is my habit to write verse. I write in my head but will also speak the words evenly to myself if nobody is near, and if competing with the wind, with asperities that inadvertently make my dog slink submissively to my side. This morning, as I was turning over the above line, remorselessly trying to find a way to connect it to a larger passage, I encountered a woman with two lurchers. I allowed myself, as I always do, a quick greeting accompanied by a smile, whilst continuing to audition the line mentally within various configurations. However, she stopped, and asked me a question and the ensuing brief conversation went like this:

"Have you seen the bluebells?"
"Yes!" I hadn't seen them. She was looking for me to elaborate. I did not know where they might be situated, and so added, "And I saw the um, the um, the winged, the er buzzcocks. What are they called?"
"The bluebells?" offered the woman, encouragingly.
The ambient line of poetry was still turning over.
"No, the, well the birds of prey."
I hadn't seen any of those either.

With differs confined to what is remembered, art unlocks nothing new –
With withdrawn mind, I appeased the past on courses connatural to
Concentrated thought, but distracted, I fabricate such wheeling birds.
Distraction makes a memory fictive through panting, faltering words,
But the colours, the colours are new, when, summoned back to this footpath,
I fabricate such wheeling birds.

Overhearing a Conversation in The Flowerpots, Cheriton

There was a power cut in the pub last night. All light but the fire's glow went
Out, and in the discontinuance, I mumbled, murmured, "Winter of Discontent",
"The 70s" and "Jeremy Corbyn", to parody the two men at
The next table, who, up until this outage, had been enjoying a chat
About the economy, each affirming the other's assertions that
All employees in the public sector are over-pensioned, indolent
And unprofitable. No one knew me well, and, excepting the fire, this veil meant
I could beard, and would satirise, bold enough not to belie the charming
Ale, as I am loath to misrepresent the pleasure I get from drinking,
With these barely-barbed rhubarbs, without fear of someone identifying
The source. Peripety-lumen, propelling the dark forward to foment
Uneasiness and consternation, my presence murmured darker yet,
excrescent.

Study of Fists II

Make a fist, its distal side between the second and third knuckles, subsided staves
Of senescence, shows that you are too old to be enigmatic.
Children early for school righting vases capriciously among the rows of graves
Use their fists to tamp.

Adopted Road

They pick at my cuff and pull a wiper from my car's tonsure,
Atrabiliar and surly, they explore me with censure.
Reason falls short, favours the non-subtle extrapolation—
To those not open to the concept of appropriation,
Someone who wears an army jacket must be in the army,
Or an impostor; and the part of the road that happens to be
Outside their house, is their own, by camber and corollary,
Not for the common; and thus they seize, when they do not get me,
Onto the cuffs, the sleeves and collar of my camouflaged smocks,
Uncomprehending of incongruous fatigues, orthodox
Of war, being worn on the school run; and when my car is parked
Outside, they act up, at dawn, undisturbed at dawn, foreheads marked
With entitlement, and they make my windscreen wiper acute.
Peaceable in isolation, I would merely institute
A basis for enlightenment, a parable to digest:
I started to help him dig his car from the snow, but left the rest
For him to disperse, alone, after he mused tentatively
That I had sound practical reasons, other than charity,
To aid; he could not puzzle it, how someone could just be kind,
Frivolously neighbourly, on this adopted road inclined
To flood, though not on my side.

Perturbation Decal

An old lady stops walking. Her hands and legs flare outwards, abducted like a skydiver's. I am watching her from my car. She is clinging to a web, wrapping her prey in fine silk, feeding herself in scoops, and then, resiled, resumes when the gust of wind that must have fixed her abates.

Mediating the Human Flesh Engine

Approaching the stationary tractor I can see through the back window and windscreen someone walking away from it:

The subaltern, Helen, whose tact is mortified to countervail chagrin in the artist who was turned a telltale tit

When he made her message public. Amanuensis of the charity she works for, and thus, like me, a conduit,

Helen had declined the offer of a limited edition print for auction, but stated, whilst they could not commit,

That an original would be considered. Helen, I write my poems under the authority of a spirit,

I am dissociated, as you are, and the vigilantes who chasten you echo those people who discomfit

Me. I watch you through the aligned windows of a tractor, heading away, through the heliotrope and hydropic grit;

And I too have been denigrated, Helen, having asked for too much on behalf of a spirit for whom I transmit.

Lines for Farkhunda

Whence water lapped within the hanging basket's parabolic earth,
I went to Nizar Qabbani's grave by quiet agency's worth.
"It come to my atair!" he trilled, to check I had not drifted off.
I drifted off to get there, but knew trough would cancel out a trough,
Rousing me that I should quaff undreaming. I was with him, and not
Of a single absent-mindedness too far, as ballast, forgot
The bench I was sitting at in Crondall, some, that I stayed lucid.
"Aphantasic in grief, I could not see, the way my mother did,
The face of my sister how it was in life. I could only see
Her distraught before her self-destruction. Come to my atair!" He
Continued: "Muslim women, from Eritrea to the Yemen
Up to England, are attacked, blamed, condescended to by Femen,
Forced and enslaved. I could only protest by sly sentiments, hid,
And criticise Arab men, though they could not be certain I did,
But you must write candidly of Farkhunda. Yes, I know that you
Feel painted, that Sitter and Subject are a quiet man, but through
Quietness, through your Apparitionism, you have agency.
No man may touch the coffin; and Farkundha's mother cannot see
Her daughter's face as it was before lapidation's wounds." Water
Laps colic in the parabolic earth. I am back, transporter,
At the Plume of Feathers, Crondall.

Care Of

It's a small world getting, while I'm eating
A bag of vinegary chips in Warwick town centre;
A small world that could change the imprint
From Paris to Sorrento, just in the telling;
And I am here to pursue a line of thought,
As my sister is meeting
An old friend of mine at Christie's.
Christkind carrying a fir tree, Hertha's altar,
Tablecloths interlarded with pathos,
The elf who makes the cracker toys, Elen Mölter;
And I am here.
It's a small world getting, but not for a seer.

Addressing Abstracts on National Poetry Day

Day dreamt up to rub it in,
Poets worth their curing salt—
Unprecedented wars thin
Your relevance. Stoppered vault—
Are these present wars too foul,
That McGough's wordplays displace
A seer's lines on the boy's bowel,
Ruined as the bombs efface
Aleppo? Tending to use
Pomegranates when she weaned,
With a sweetness to infuse
Till munitions supervened,
His mother had held him nearest her,
Her heart's continuity
Assuring his viscera,
And then turned, that his ear be
Less orbital of her breast,
And yet equable virtues convened
As if it remained there, pressed,
Till munitions supervened.

Sowas

My dog is farting, and each time I open the door, as the lone dispenser of sweets this Halloween, I am inadvertently conveying the smell to the children in the porch.

Conjuncture

Semi-solitary in the courtyard of our holiday cottage, I put my book down for a moment to look up at High Wheeldon. My hair is like a clown's, my oversized yellow hiking boots are like a clown's; you might visualise the paraphernalia, car collapsing around me, squirty flower. There is a woman sitting reading in the next courtyard along, the mother of the little girl my daughter has made friends with. I have spoken with her, but not very much.

A gust of wind makes the pages of my book flicker open on the table and one of my various bookmarks separates and escapes over the low partitioning stone wall between the courtyards.

Over the years, my children have prolifically written messages on small scraps of paper, or drawn pictures, and not having the heart to dispose of them, I tend to pool together all those of a period coinciding with my allegiance to a particular book, using the burgeoning wad to mark my progress.

I instantly wonder which herald has been blown over the wall, now adhering to the ankle of the woman reading quietly, entreating her to glance down. I hope it is just a drawing and not the message, which I know to be among them, left on my pillow several weeks ago (I have been reading this novel since then) by my daughter, which states "I Love You."

In My Family's Midst

In my family's midst, the wag isolates me. He jokes, says that he fears his daughter has inherited my mother's ugly genes, that my seven-year-old son looks like President Putin, and calls teasingly, "Hey, Vladimir," in the direction of the boy playing on the floor with his car track. My son, not conversant with heads of state, lines up cars on the starting gate, unaware that he is being addressed, mocked; my objecting vociferously would compromise that, and so I say nothing.

Age, old age, has aimed at me. It was a collision intended.

Later, I got into my car and sat there alone for a few moments with my head down, holding my temples, and looking up to my left noticed the next car along was moving gently forward from its parking space. No. No, I was moving backwards. I had taken the handbrake off and I could not remember doing so. And so I drove back home and fell onto my bed and slept, and woke up delirious, not knowing what time it was, nor did staring at the time on the clock give me clarity, and I heard a voice outside on the street, young and lucid, and I felt frightened, vulnerable in my confusion.

Metanoia

Cunctator, contrite,
Entering each decade
Sooner than he might,
Resists in retrograde
His growth's advising,
Is still, with grace delayed,
Self-aggrandising.
Repentance that put paid
To relapsing pride
Indentures, but has made
Him near-edified.

The Snake

Institutions circumscribe the geofamilial lee,
Wonder immanent to a child is proclaimed more narrowly,
And elided from earnest expression when their lungs will take
But rules, phlogiston, within coils constitutive of the snake.

Attuned to Haintune or Hartland, we escape the retardant
Effect of the snake, watchful snake without eyelids, regardant
Without shoulder, yet stay, as when wakeful, within its purview.
When someone is behind me, following, though not to pursue,

I like to create illusions, abrupt transitions in my wake –
In moments when they have lost sight of me, at a curve, I make
Distance, fluctuant, running but then resuming an apt pace
Before they cease to be blinded and see me there, out of place,

Too far ahead; but my improbable progress, elected,
Is assimilated perforce, and would seem quite expected
After sense is soothed according to that need in all of us,
Personified at Hartland Quay, where a baboon's proboscis

Ever ameliorates the recumbent woman's ague
By resting against her hair. She is sense. And the snake's purview,
Not seeing dreams of Haintune, or Hartland out of its range,
Questions our unlikely headway before accepting the change.

Wonder immanent to a child, in mimetoliths, immense;
See what we can get away with when the snake defers to sense.

Immense

My seven-year-old son is in his red sleeping bag. I am lying next to him on an airport floor. Sun is streaming in through the giant window that gives onto the runways. The sun here never sets. We are playing a game, calling each other scatological names, and my son is laughing his laugh. "OK, time to go to sleep." My little boy instantly snuggles down, closing his eyes, but then I see his pronated hand. I put my hand flat upon it. "I am here, son." He sleeps. It is simple, nothing is simile, nothing is like anything else, or as such as such, and the sun streams in through the window.

News of Roodias's Death Prompts me to Consider Empathy's Shortcomings

Immortality sustained by regime is irrelevant when people still die
unguarded, violently, having imbibed crystal meth after the label on the
bottle had led them to believe that it was a health drink. Those people who
yet die swiftly, too swiftly for meaningful intervention, the "I am in trouble
here, I am dying, I am dead", are the only ones left in need of psychopomps
to guide them to an afterlife. His family were from Goa, descended from
Portuguese seafarers, and Roodias had a catholic funeral in Milton,
Cambridge, a rood suspended by wires above the catafalque.

My ability to feel empathy is outpacing my literary prowess;
Whilst the poplar trees extending yonder in a row on my left seem to
coalesce,
When I cut diagonally across this same field, ahead of my expectation,
And the point at which they have pivoted to appear, in profile, as a
venation
Of trunks and boughs, as if belonging to one, comes sooner on the path
each day. Elan
Of empathy draws Roodias expediently into the closed hand fan,
The scabrous guardsticks, of these poplars, and the inference there, before
me in the blear,
Is of my father, his death prefigured – it is he who says "I am in trouble
here,
I am dying, I am dead." What virtue is in empathy that obscures Roodias,
In honed empathy for others when it is expeditiously gleaned of the bias
Towards my father, or myself? I must establish a sorrow with fidelity
To Roodias, peculiar, and his being, his face, essence, unpollarded, see,
Procrastinate, attentive, beyond the coalescence to scrutinise the rearmost
Poplars. He was my landlord when I was living in Histon. Whenever I
burned toast,
The smoke alarm would go off in his Indian restaurant, which was situated
Below my flat. Sometimes, it went off randomly, weeks after the smoke had
abated,
And Roodias became obsessed, coming round every night to inspect the
alarm.
He was lovely, intelligent, but would talk incoherently, and this was his
charm
And also what left me exasperated, until one day, when I was at work in
The library, my fury rose like a dragon with the jaws of a slumped salt-grit
bin,

And I confess now to having visualised doing him harm, punching him as he,
In my imagination, was yet again standing on a chair, assiduously
Removing the alarm's housing. Later, when I arrived home, I found that the bathroom
Mirror had fallen and smashed on the floor. Roodias then came with a dustpan and broom,
And I felt guilty as he helped me tidy up the shards, pondering the evidence
Of telekinesis. Had my raving thoughts, in contrast now with the gentleness
Of our picking up of black-backed glass, made this happen? And then Roodias touched my hand,
And said, jokingly, as if amorous, "Oh Rogan." I laughed, though after, he would stand
On the chair, talking accusingly about toast. What merit has empathy—
"The cork
Under the cap should alert you, Roodias," is what I say to myself as I walk
Despondently away from the poplars, then, "Why did you drink it; after admitting
To your daughter that it tasted so awful, why did you persist?"

Document of Vehement Verbigeration

"Ooh aah Cantona": stifling a curse, I tend to say this when I am physically hurt in a child's company (reserved for modest pain, e.g. on burning myself on a baking tray, snagging my hand on a thorn or stubbing my toe on a bed leg).

"ZZ Top": I say this when, for the last time, exhausted and exasperated, I tell the kids to go to bed, reinforcing the command with a non-verbal cue (with my elbows on the axle of my abdomen, swivelling my arms to point my fingers in the direction of their bedroom).

"Oh Matron": something I say in a sordid manner when I am finally going to the toilet after holding it in for too long.

"Ooh Crosse and Blackwell": I invariably say this when I am in the process of fitting either myself or my car through a narrow opening.

For Woo, Who Made Me Milk With Cloves

A private sensation—
Explosions that inhere
In the indentation
And sacral diapir
Above my bum crack, where
The buttocks' contours let,
And a pocket of air
Formed between in the sweat,
Once risen, egresses;
This private sensation
Is felt, effervesces
To mark the privation
Of awareness of it,
But could fizz like Cava,
Still I, like a spirit
Barred from his cadaver,
Benighted, may not know
Sensations inside you.

Notes for a poem set in Gostrey Meadow

I tease one of my wife's long blonde hairs from my urethra.
Litotes, they are not scarce, but abound in the owls' nests.
Outside of my tradition, in the caesura era,
I mistook a woman's forearms for elongated breasts,
And the sleeves at her elbows for a neckline, as she sat
On the opposite bank; but I observed discreetly, while
Crossing the bridge to get to these public toilets, how that
Upper section of flesh was hesitantly prehensile,
That she was simply resting elbows on her knees, chin on her
Hands. Not wishing to objectify her, or yield ribald
To postmodernism, this, in the caesura era,
Was how it was; fishermen fished, though nothing nibbled
Once my kids started throwing a ball into the water;
As I left, my dog, shaking, was making my family
Wet on the far bank, while the woman's husband and daughter
Played nearby, and she sat with her palms, soon patently,
Holding her head; and at this threshold, a rainbow
Manifested in droplets ejected from my dog's fur.
I extricate my wife's hair, wonder what I might yet know,
Living among the ivied fork, adumbration of her
In the owls' nests; with this sensation, inaudible squeak
Of unravelling ixtle twine, something cloaked astray
In prestidigitation makes this cubicle space streak
In penumbra. I leave, running back to the River Wey,
And in a specular scene, from which, as I draw nearer,
I see my family are missing, the woman is still there,
And I feel that she wants to say, "The caesura era
Is over," but is too reserved or dumbfounded to swear
To it. But I sense that all digital data is lost.
Untwined from the line of poets, but for hard copy notes
And marginalia hastily handwritten and tossed
On the sill or secreted presciently in my coat's
Pocket, I am dumb, or dictate in darkness, half awake
In reverie, so history finds me incoherent.
Dye of my work would not to posterity's textiles take,
But beggar archives by a binary, non-adherent.

The Bifurcation

Near to the Hampshire border and beyond the bifurcation
Are narratives of given names with virtue's connotation
Or championing the status to which parents might aspire;
Charity and Christian, oddly wistful for the empire,
Call their daughter India, India of revanche.
And as Pankridge Street in Hampshire links to heedless roads that branch
Off to Surrey, they will straddle obligations to their names
And self-interest.

Effaced Between Sherril and Babeny

Minority isolationists preponderate democratically
Over those of global art fairs and financial interfaces,
Over those who protest "Refugees are welcome" but, covertly, inwardly,
Brook no pressure on school places.

Fealty

There is a Royal willy-holder, and he has a Royal willy-holder's willy-holder, and he has a Royal willy-holder's willy-holder's willy-holder and so on, and when you see them all in silhouette on a hill, going for a wee, the sun behind them, they do look silly.

The male is one aspect on the feudal strewnfields of relief, where, in fief, the serf holds the villein holding the freeman holding the squire holding the film censor; and as they watch seven hours of paint drying by Charlie Lyne, the other just squats and leaves.

The Amateur Hermeneutist

The self-styled world-weary and woke
Poetry book reviewer
Asserts tartly that I invoke
The worst a hermeneur
May bring to his note, by decree,
That states "no cishet white men".
Aided by a dichotomy
Between discrimination when
It is merely consumer choice
And when it involves oppression,
He expatiates with the voice
Of one whose pained confession
Is that he himself is "cishet".

Leap Year

The notion of someone eating is lachrymose in me, induces tears,
On this day, intercalary, compensative of costive solar years;
Educes the contraband, empathy, that Wilde was too coy to declare,
Euphemistically calling it "genius"; the same milestones-aware
That Morrissey possesses, though it was not concealed down his rear
cleavage,
Where the TSA agent imposed his finger. Each poet must manage
Their own way to empathy – mine is through the notion of someone eating.
Nutation of the axis pangs, my sense of it mounts; I hear scurrying,
See shadows of ectomorphs fleeing, hear snarling parley in the graveyard,
Sense nutation of the axis, note, at Yarl's Wood, the sub-threshold saccade
Of a woman's eyes as she threatens to throw herself from the banister.
I am the wretched migrant this leap year, the lumpenproletarier
That so many liberals, whilst refuting that I would drive wages down,
Uphold by precept, endear by poiesis, allow by praxis to drown
Or be detained at Yarl's Wood (the guards joke of headbutting the women
there,
Of walking into the rooms unannounced, because they are "breast men"),
to where
I evanesce by my empathy to be one of the Adventitious.

Paradox (dual lines beside Swinburne's grave)

I needed to write to feel rejected and thereby have something to write about,
But my fluency, provisional until people follow,
Mounts when they respond, even when migraine wrecks that purchasing gwick in my swallow;
And reconciling rejection with recognition I hear my daughter cry out
"Papa!" in the night. There is such fear in her voice: "I dreamt you were pushing the swing
Without me in the seat, and it was swinging round the bar hitting you on the head.
Each time you were hit you looked at me, Papa, like you were getting more bewildered."

The swing's seat by sudden discontinuities in its revolutions, jouncing
And catapulting into my head, is my conceit, Swinburne,
(The gravestone looks askance,) excessive applications of treatment for scalp ringworm
To jaundice myself, so that I may feel like I am inexorably nearing
Death (the lobed hilt of its carved sword holding the atheist in a sacred redoubt);
But my knowing that I can cease treatment and presently be safely delivered
Precludes me from capitalising on concentrated thought. Merely bewildered,
I am merely bewildered.
        (In locus below the ledger's tang, bones may not hear me,
        Nor pressed primroses to press-gang a heathen's corpse)

71

Lines by a Precariat on Culture and Religion

I mentioned God, and I lost them.
I bought a dog tag from a surplus store in Fareham;
The blood type on the dog tag may or may not match mine;
The religious preference may or may not be mine.

Covert believer, coquettish with an image of himself as atheist,
Was given disbelief during transfusion
And went into shock.

I'm "N", am noon for Nasrani,
On my window smooth as sea glass, etched to expose me.
I'm bloody-minded enough not to replace the pane:
If you think you're hard enough, Isis, if you think you're hard enough.

Is, isn't, pardie, seeing how the frog
Straddles both in an ikizukuri
Parody, its eyes blinking ardently
And abruptly, I should remove to hate
All culture, for does it not subjugate
Me, in my gaze confuse what existed
And what exists yet? Am I not listed
On the paranormal database, like
Those moon-heeled sylphs who witnesses claim strike
Out for the bank only to hang reposed
Above the stream? The virtue thus proposed
As advisable, by implicature,
To remove in order to hate culture
Is tolerance; and as I walk my dog
This evening, passing households in a ward
Claimed by the Tories, and feeling ignored,
I could almost join them in their mistrust
Of others; but then glancing up, and just
In the moments it takes me to walk by,
I see through a window a girl that I
Know to be eight or nine, for she is in
My daughter's school year, and a more sanguine
Appraisal of existence, reconciled
With tolerance and all ideals compiled
Within grace's fardel, forms in my mind.
Alone in her bedroom, how mild, how kind
She seems, looking pensively into her

Dressing mirror, holding what I infer
To be a hairbrush. What is she thinking?
She was not here 10 years ago. I bring
My dog, Larkin, to heel, and I am passed,
Part precariat, part iconoclast.
What is there but that I am not heeded,
What is there but that I am not needed?
There is a paternal streak from afar.

Logic Distractors and Salvors

Of that that a rose's gyres and fetches bring to its contours,
Of roseness relinquished, I am apparition brought to you.
Of that that quiddity surrenders of itself, I am yours.
Someone talked of me, advised someone else to urge me to slew
My telescope to nearer aspects, and, scarce, I glimpsed myself
In the demi-plasma that surrounds the rose, and that would prove
To be the last allusion; and I take quinoa from the shelf,
And that will be my last meal, and I will till a tender groove
With my fork, pour in apple cider vinegar, and no one
Will see me swallow like a child; the last allusion to me,
Adamantine, the last allusion to concrete "whatness". None
Shall speak of me again.

November Decals

My isolation is invidious;
Further isolation is imposed as a sanction.
My oxymoronic indigenous
16th-Galway-hair, ne'er avulsed by English traction,
Disconcerts.

In spite of sumptuary officials sent to verify verse written for tacit
readerships,
I write for a muse, eccedentesiast, whose eyes do not smile at me in accord
with his lips
But are frightened and minatory, seeming to say, "Away, no one asked you
to write about me,"
While faithful to that other muse who is not a subject, the one who has
come to me divinely.

As those with stammers, to obviate disfluency, audition words before
stating what they want,
And are thus learning new ways, words, syntax, new things they desire, in
procrustean kerning of font,
I tune rhyme into a state of proper harmony. Poetry is a revelation of what
I desire and what I praise and oppugn, for a muse who is subject, and by a
muse who is not.

The Life Review

Encountered on the trail:
A grey enenra pall,
A glinting Hilti nail,
A pug, the dog du jour;
And all the children quail
At tympanic pumpkins.

These images assail
My mind and yet withal
Enprehension detail—
Quicksilver the allure
Of each before they pale
And the last block begins.

www.ingramcontent.com/pod-product-compliance
Lightning Source LLC
Chambersburg PA
CBHW060529030426
42337CB00021B/4199